BRITAIN IN OLD PH

Musselburgh

THE OLD MUSSELBURGH CLUB

SUTTON PUBLISHING LIMITED

Sutton Publishing Limited
Phoenix Mill · Thrupp · Stroud
Gloucestershire · GL5 2BU

First published 2000

Reprinted in 2001

Title page photograph: The Mall looking
across the river to Eskside West with the
Roman bridge in the foreground and the
Mitchell Street tenements behind, *c.* 1958.

British Library Cataloguing in Publication Data
A catalogue record for this book is available from the
British Library.

ISBN 0-7509-2531-0

Typeset in 10.5/13.5 Photina.
Typesetting and origination by
Sutton Publishing Limited.
Printed and bound in England by
J.H. Haynes & Co. Ltd, Sparkford.

A four-view postcard and the Musselburgh coat of arms, 1913.

CONTENTS

ACKNOWLEDGEMENTS

The Old Musselburgh Club is grateful to the undernoted for their encouragement, assistance and generosity:

East Lothian Council Library Service
The Staff of Musselburgh Library
Musselburgh Museum Committee
The copyright holders
John Hislop and Bryden Stillie for their computing services
Those townspeople who so kindly lent photographs from their collections.

The Club also acknowledges the research carried out by the authors of the following publications:

W.C. Maughan and George Colville, *Picturesque Musselburgh and its Golf Links*, Alexander Gardner, Paisley, 1906; reprinted by Colville Books, Musselburgh, 1985
George Colville, *5 Open Champions and the Musselburgh Golf Story*, Colville Books, Musselburgh, 1980
Brian W. Heeps, *In Beauty Enshrined*, Brian W. Heeps, 1989
Donald Lindgren, *Musselburgh in Old Picture Postcards*, European Library, vols 1–3, 1989–95
East Lothian Community History and Arts Trust, *The Way We Were in Musselburgh and Fisherrow*, ELCHAT

David Stillie
The Old Musselburgh Club

The High Street, 1827. (*East Lothian Council*)

PREFACE

This book takes a nostalgic look at the Burgh of Musselburgh as it was during the late nineteenth century and up to the Riding of the Marches in 1974. The town changed quite considerably during that time and much of the industry, many family businesses, hospitals, schools and even streets, which once were so familiar, have disappeared. They are but a memory, or the subject of conversation for the older generation. This publication is intended to rekindle these long-forgotten memories and to allow the younger generation, perhaps for the first time, an insight into what the town was like all those years ago. We must be thankful for the art of photography and the part it has played in capturing moments when time literally stood still and which were recorded on film for all time.

This issue has been compiled, to celebrate the millennium, by members of The Old Musselburgh Club, an organisation dedicated to preserving the ancient customs and institutions of the town, its history and traditions and to fostering local art and literature. The Club chose as its mentor David McBeth Moir (1798–1851), a respected citizen, a caring and diligent physician and a poet and writer of outstanding ability.

The Club crest incorporates his 'signature', namely the letter 'M' enclosed in a circle pierced by an arrow.

The Club has been assisted by many organisations but the magnificent response from the townsfolk who have searched through attics and outhouses for previously unpublished material has helped the Club create this wonderfully graphic story of the burgh. I hope that this glimpse of bygone days will bring back fond memories.

A. Hogg
President,
The Old Musselburgh Club

Musselburgh Town Council just before the First World War. Standing, left to right: Cllr Tait, Baillie Gibb, Ex-Provost Simpson, Cllr Young, Cllr Downie; seated: Baillie Niven, Cllr Dobbie, Ex-Provost Constable, Provost Miller, Baillie Miller, Cllr Bourhill, Town Clerk John Richardson.

The town hall, 1912. (*Jackson Collection [DC111] by permission of Glasgow University Archives & Business Record Centre*)

INTRODUCTION: THE STORY OF MUSSELBURGH

'Musselburgh was a burgh when Edinburgh was nane,
And Musselburgh will be a burgh when Edinburgh's gane.'
'The Musselburgh Song', Alex Innes, 1935

Musselburgh is one of the oldest and most historic burghs in Scotland and its origins can be traced back some 3,000 years to the Bronze Age. It was the Romans who first realised the strategic importance of the area and in the second century AD they built a station at Inveresk on the land now occupied by the Parish Kirk of St Michael and Musselburgh Grammar School. To supply their garrison at Inveresk they constructed a harbour, near the modern harbour at Fisherrow, and bridged the River Esk. To this day the Roman bridge still spans the river, uniting the communities of Fisherrow and Musselburgh. The Roman occupation, however, was simply the prelude to a rich and enthralling history which mirrors the story that is Scotland.

In earlier times tribal cults worshipped the pagan god of light at Inveresk but the area finally became a centre of Christian worship when St Modwenna founded the first St Michael's Church on top of Inveresk Hill. The original building is said to have been constructed of mud and wattle and was thatched with reeds from the Shirehaugh, a far cry from the present imposing Parish Kirk of St Michael. There is a link with the past, however, as it is said that some of the present stonework was taken from the Roman fortifications. The influence of St Modwenna still lingers on in the churches of many denominations found in and around the town.

The lands, mills and fishing grounds adjacent to the town were once owned by the monks of Dunfermline Abbey whose abbot chose to live in Pinkie Tower, later to become Pinkie House, which was, for many years, the home of the much-respected Hope family. This historic building is now owned by the world famous Loretto School.

The ancient burgh, through its proximity to Edinburgh, has witnessed the full pageantry of Scottish history and even the town's motto is part of that story. In July 1332 the Regent of Scotland, the Earl of Moray, died in the town after a long illness, during which time he was cared for by the people of Musselburgh. When his successor, the Earl of Mar, offered to reward the townspeople for their kindness, they declined, saying that they were only doing their duty. The Regent was so impressed that he described them as 'Honest Men' and since then Musselburgh has been known as the 'Honest Toun' with the word 'Honesty' incorporated into the Coat of Arms.

The town has twice suffered the indignity of being burned down by the English, who also inflicted a disastrous defeat on the Scots, just south of the town, at the Battle of Pinkie in 1547. The battle has been described as the bloodiest battle in Scottish history and it is recorded that, for several days following the battle, the Pinkie Burn ran red with the blood of the defeated Scots. Just above the battlefield, on Carberry Hill, Mary Queen of Scots surrendered to the confederate lords in 1567. In 1650 Cromwell's army camped on Musselburgh Links and incurred the

An aerial view looking south-west along Musselburgh High Street towards the Rver Esk and Fisherrow with the town hall in the centre and showing the Roman bridge, the Rennie bridge and the footbridge linking North High Street, Fisherrow, to Millhill, 1963. (*Scotsman Publications*)

An aerial view looking down river, with Fisherrow on the left bank and Musselburgh on the right, 1963. The railway station is in the centre and from left to right along the coast are Fisherrow Links, Loretto School's playing fields at Newfield and Musselburgh Racecourse. (*Scotsman Publications*)

displeasure of the local people by stabling his horses in St Michael's Church. Bonnie Prince Charlie stayed at Pinkie House after his victory at the Battle of Prestonpans in 1745 and later, during the Napoleonic Wars, troops once again bivouacked on Musselburgh Links and barracks were built near Pinkie Road. Fishermen from the town volunteered to defend the coast against a possible French invasion and, for their loyalty, were presented with a medal by the County of Midlothian. To this day the medal is worn by the President of the Fishermen's Association as he leads the Fishermen's Walk through the town.

Coal mining was one of the main occupations in the area and many of the villages around Musselburgh were dependent on the 'local' colliery for employment. For many years the factories of J. & W. Stuart and Brunton's of Musselburgh manufactured fishing nets and wire for customers around the world. During both world wars wire was produced at Brunton's for ships, aircraft and barrage balloons and one of their last commissions in peacetime was to supply wire for the suspension cables of the Forth Road Bridge at South Queensferry. Unfortunately, the demise of the fishing industry and the reduction in demand for steel wire caused both factories to close but in their day they led the world in production and in expertise. Brewing, market gardening, cotton, paper-making, tanning and golf-club manufacture were some of the other industries that brought prosperity and fame to the town but they, too, have gone and the once flourishing fishing industry is but a shadow of its former self.

Musselburgh has always had a reputation for sporting excellence, catering for such diverse tastes as archery, football, rugby, athletics and horse racing, but it will forever be associated with the origins and development of the game of golf. Golf was first played over Musselburgh Links in 1672 which makes the course one of the oldest in the country and, indeed, there are those who will argue that it is the oldest in the land. The open championship was held at Musselburgh on six occasions between 1872 and 1891 and the town, in addition to providing the championship course, also produced many fine golfers including five open champions. Horse racing has been held on the Links since 1817, when such meetings were transferred from Leith Sands, near Edinburgh, to Musselburgh. The Royal Company of Archers shoot annually over the same Links for the Musselburgh Silver Arrow, which is reputed to be the oldest sporting trophy in the world that is still the subject of regular competition.

The people of Musselburgh take great pride in the past glories and achievements of the town but, at the same time, have a tremendous enthusiasm for the future. This is typified by both the Riding of the Marches, which is held every twenty-one years, and the Musselburgh Festival. The Riding of the Marches can be traced back officially to 1682, although it probably took place for centuries before that, and is a symbolic ceremony of riding the boundaries of the town and claiming them anew for the people of Musselburgh. The festival is held on each of the intervening years and the town elects an Honest Lad and Lass who are charged not only to keep the old traditions alive but also to promote pride in the town as it is today and to strengthen the sense of community for the future. These events offer a time for renewing old friendships, for reliving old memories and for taking part in the continuing story of the 'Honest Toun'.

A. Hogg
President, The Old Musselburgh Club

1

Street Scenes

The northern boundary of the town follows the shore of the Firth of Forth from the Magdalene Burn in the west to the Ravensheugh Burn in the east. Almost midway between these points the River Esk joins the Forth and this physical barrier led to the town developing into two distinct and separate communities: the fishing community of Fisherrow on the east bank of the river and the industrial areas of Musselburgh on the west bank. The construction of the road bridge in the late nineteenth century brought both communities together and the town expanded southwards towards Inveresk and Monktonhall. Large-scale house building in the second half of the twentieth century cleared much of the older fabric of the town and created the townscape we know today.

Levenhall and West Pans, 1914. This area on the east boundary of the town has now disappeared under the Cockenzie Power Station ash lagoons. The four lagoons cover the whole seafront from the mouth of the River Esk to the boundary with Prestonpans and have added a large area of recreational land on the seaward side of Musselburgh Racecourse.

Musselburgh High Street looking east, 1904. St Peter's Episcopal Church stands to the right of Pinkie Pillars with the Commercial Hotel on the left. Traces of Roman stonework from Inveresk can be seen in Pinkie Pillars, which were constructed in 1707.

Musselburgh High Street looking west, 1904. This photograph shows the cab office and horse-drawn cabs that carried Edinburgh golfers from the railway station to Musselburgh Links.

The Mercat Cross and Musselburgh Arms Hotel from the town hall, *c.* 1905. The wide street was formed when Mid Row was demolished in the nineteenth century.

High Street looking west towards the High Church tower with an electric tram run by the Musselburgh Light and Power Company, *c.* 1910. Musselburgh's electric trams were in service for a number of years before the Edinburgh cable trams system was electrified, forcing passengers for Edinburgh to change at Joppa. The buildings on the left were demolished to make way for the new Bank of Scotland.

The town hall and the old clock, 1850s. The clock was presented to Musselburgh by Dutch merchants from Veere in 1446 and was replaced with the present clock in 1873. The original clock is one of only a few of its kind still in existence, and is on display in the foyer of the town hall. (*The Cavaye Collection of Thomas Begbie Prints*)

High Street looking east, 1906. From the lack of traffic it is hard to believe that until the 1990s this street was part of the A1 trunk road linking Edinburgh to London. Although many of the shopfronts have altered, there has been little change in the scale of the buildings themselves, with the exception of the new Musselburgh & Fisherrow Co-operative Society store on the site of the three-storey tenement to the left of the tram.

High Street looking east from the High Church tower showing the lade and the old mill with the Hollies, formerly the council offices, the Burgh School and in the background the chimneys of the Sea Mill and the gas works, *c.* 1908.

The island site at the junction of Hercus Loan and South Street, with Bessie Thomas' shop and Andrew Young on the bicycle (right) selling ice-cream for Rapallini of New Street, 1940s. (*Florence Howie*)

Newbigging/Inveresk Road, 1950s. This photograph shows the buildings opposite the Horseshoe just before demolition. The building on the far left still stands in front of the new swimming pool and sports centre next to Musselburgh Grammar School. (*East Lothian Council*)

Carberry Road, Inveresk village, *c.* 1910. This terrace of cottages and townhouses has been extensively renovated since this photograph was taken. French the blacksmith's premises have been converted to a house and a small shop occupies the ground floor of the adjoining two-storey building. (*Crown Copyright RCAHMS*)

James Street/Millhill, 1950s. All the buildings on the left, back to where the car is parked, were demolished in the early 1950s to provide new housing and Millhill has been re-aligned at its junction with James Street. (*East Lothian Council*)

The Mall, 1930s. The Mall lies along the banks of the Esk between the Rennie bridge and the Roman bridge. The Central Picture House stood on the site now occupied by the former Eastern Scottish bus garage.

The Mall, 1906. The mill lade, the mill dam, which provided water power to the numerous mills in the town, was open as it ran through the town by way of High Street, Dambrae, Millhill to Goosegreen, where it re-entered the river.

Wash day at the Roman bridge, 1850s. Lilybank House stands behind the cottages in Eskside West. (*The Cavaye Collection of Thomas Begbie Prints*)

The Mall looking across the river to Eskside West with the Roman bridge in the foreground and the Mitchell Street tenements behind, *c.* 1958. The Roman bridge is of medieval construction and stands on the site of the original Roman causeway below their camp at Inveresk. (*J.T. Knight*)

A Loretto School boat race on the Esk, looking down river to the 'Store' bridge at the east end of North High Street.

At Newfield a Loretto pupil crosses the old footbridge from the Newfield buildings to the main school on the east side of the river, 1950s. (*Loretto School*)

Flooding in Eskside West between the Roman bridge and the Rennie bridge, 21 September 1891.

North High Street, Fisherrow, 1910. The original Hayweights building can be seen in the centre of the photograph, behind the horse-drawn bus.

North High Street, late 1930s. Note the clock and new roof on the Hayweights. The Hayweights and the buildings to the right were demolished in the 1960s to make way for Brunton Hall. This was an ambitious project by Musselburgh Town Council, funded by a bequest from the local industrialist John Brunton, to provide function halls, a 300-seat theatre, courts and council offices.

West Holmes Gardens soon after construction, 1900. This charming red sandstone development of houses for rent was built by Cooper Brothers Builders, who developed similar schemes in Inveresk Road and Monktonhall Terrace.

New Street, 1905. In the heart of the fishing community of Fisherrow, New Street runs from the harbour to the Esk and at one time coal was carried by horse-drawn railway from the mines at Pinkie to the harbour by this route. Fisherrow Yacht Club now occupies the building on the left.

Fisherrow harbour. Although no longer an active fishing port, the harbour is full of leisure craft and still holds the same attraction for children.

The Promenade at Fisherrow from the harbour wall with pleasure boats for hire, c. 1900. The high roof at the rear is part of John Anderson & Company's Bush Brewery which closed in 1877.

2

At Work

There is a long tradition of coal mining and market gardening in and around Musselburgh, but with the founding of J. & W. Stuart's cotton twine and net mill in 1859, Inveresk papermill in 1860 and Brunton's wiremill in 1870, the scene was set for the rapid development of the town. All three of these companies developed international reputations not only for the quality of their products but also for their evolution of new production techniques. These major employers have now closed or have moved to other sites away from the town, and in recent years new businesses have taken over the redeveloped sites. They continue, in their own way, the industrial heritage of the town.

An aerial photograph of the main factories along the banks of the Esk, *c.* 1972. Left to right: Brunton's wiremill, Stuart's net and twine factory and the Inveresk papermill. Inveresk village is at the top left with Monktonhall Golf Club nestling in a loop of the river. The light areas bottom right are glasshouses at Stoneyhill Farm. (*Scotsman Publications*)

Wire hawser winding machines at Brunton's wiremill. (*Brunton's*)

Mooring cables for the *Queen Mary* en route to John Brown's, Clydebank, 1935. (*Brunton's*)

The 100-ton testing rig in the ropery, Brunton's wiremill. These long, narrow buildings can be clearly seen in the aerial photograph on p. 25. (*Crown Copyright RCAHMS*)

A 20,000-ft continuous tramway cable coiled on four carts leaving the factory on the first stage of its journey to Sydney, Australia, 1938. (*Brunton's*)

On a very windy night during the winter of 1951 a fire started in Brunton's wire drawing shop and spread through the engineers', electricians' and joiners' shops completely destroying the main offices and all of the company's original paperwork. The company was forced to rely on the honesty of its customers in paying their outstanding bills and its suppliers in providing copies of invoices they had rendered. Spectators can be seen standing on the Roman bridge with the railway station on the right. (*Scotsman Publications*)

Women tending spinning frames in the cotton mill at Stuart's. (*J. & W. Stuart*)

Women inspecting cotton fishing nets sometime before the First World War. (*J. & W. Stuart*)

Inspecting nets in the late 1950s. (*J.T. Knight*)

A group of workers at the loading bay at Inveresk papermill, 1950s.

Mrs Scarlett showing members of the WRAF around the market garden at Sweethope in the early 1940s. The Scarletts made a very significant contribution to the development of new plant strains.

Planting tatties at Pinkie Braes, *c.* 1958. Market gardens and arable farming still flourish in what is now part of the Edinburgh 'Green Belt'. (*East Lothian Council*)

Postal workers attending a presentation at the post office, 1930s. (*C. & F. McKean*)

Workers at Whitelaw's Brewery, with Col Whitelaw just left of centre, wearing a Homburg hat. Whitelaw's was one of at least three breweries in Fisherrow, along with Anderson's in Bush Street, which closed in 1877, and Young's, makers of the famous 'Wee Heavy', which ceased trading from their premises next to the Co-op in North High Street in the late 1960s.

The town officer with the original fifteenth-century town-hall clock prior to its being put on display in the foyer of the town hall. The movement is reputed to be the oldest in Scotland.

Mine rescue team. Coal mining has been important to the local economy for hundreds of years, from the drift mines at Pinkie, operated by the monks of Dunfermline Abbey, to the recently closed deep mine at Monktonhall. Monktonhall Colliery extended beneath the town and out under the Firth of Forth.

The interior of part of Musselburgh gas works, which was situated on the seaward side of the racecourse in Balcarres Road. The site was finally cleared in the 1980s.

Collecting mussels. The extensive mussel beds off Fisherrow not only provided bait for the line fishing but also supplied the mussel sellers, who peddled them as 'fast food' on the streets of Edinburgh.

Gilbey Brunton's, 1970. Honest Lad Reno DiRollo and Honest Lass Elise Whittaker receiving a presentation from the staff during a visit to the factory. (*Ron Taylor Studio*)

J. & J. Mitchell (Newhailes) Ltd. Newhailes mink farm was established in 1947 and traded for almost forty years. It was one of the foremost mink farms in the world, with over 12,000 mink, and exported to the USSR, China, Japan, Korea and the USA. (*Colin Ramsey*)

3

Fishing

The fisheries of Musselburgh are mentioned in the Charter granted to the Abbey of Dunfermline some ten centuries ago. The oyster and extensive mussel beds continued to provide an income for the townspeople for many centuries until over-fishing and pollution from the expanding industries along the banks of the River Esk brought this to an end. Until fairly recently a significant part of the community of Fisherrow was still 'at the fishing'. The harbour was busy until the introduction of quotas as a result of joining the Common Market. This was followed in 1984 by a ban on fishing for sprats, which brought to an end the long history of Fisherrow as an important fishing harbour. Those Fisherrow men still fishing were forced to invest in much larger boats, which are too big for this tidal harbour, and now carry on the proud fishing tradition of Fisherrow from other east-coast harbours.

Fifies and yawls lying along the west wall of Fisherrow harbour.

The gospel ship was a feature of almost every fishing family home.

'Oor Ain Fishwives'. This postcard, showing the fish market at Fisherrow harbour, was sent from Prestonpans Haddingtonshire in 1919.

Fishwives preparing fish for sale, 1876.

Fisherrow, 1870s. A busy scene in Watt's Close, showing preparations for the line fishing with the traditional reels, skulls and baskets. The houses had large stores at ground level with living accommodation above. Note the fish drying on hooks by the door.

Mrs Wallace, with a full creel of mussels, returning over Fisherrow sands at low tide.

Fishwives, left to right: Mrs Glen, Mrs Wood, Mrs Gibson and Mrs Brown – with their creels and skulls at Newhaven market. This building has now been converted to create the Newhaven Heritage Museum and a branch of Harry Ramsden's fish restaurant.

This large sailing vessel was brought into Fisherrow to be broken up in the days before the east breakwater was extended.

Left to right: Rob Thorburn snr, Walter Brown, Robert Thorburn jnr, Andrew Gibson and Edward Ritchie overhauling their boat before setting off for Stornoway and the herring fishing, late 1930s. (*A. Grier*)

The Fisherrow fleet at the mouth of Fisherrow harbour, 1953.

Robert Hope and his son Robert preparing the *Better Hope* for the herring fishing season, 1948. (*A. Grier*)

'Barking' or tanning nets at Fisherrow.

Jimmy Gibson and Duncan Blackley landing a fine catch of herring.

4

The Riding of the Marches

T he Riding of the Marches has its roots in the fifth century when the boundaries of the town were checked on a regular basis to ensure that they had not been 'adjusted' by adjoining landowners. The early processions were of a religious nature but they later became civic ceremonies as the influence of the Reformed Church increased. The earliest written record of the Riding of the Marches is contained in a minute of the town council dated 1682. The ceremonies take place every twenty-one years and at each of the twelve traditional points on the boundary the turf cutter casts a turf into the air with the shout 'It's a' oor ain'. The following day a large procession showing the 'Life of the Town' takes place.

Town Champion John Downie (on horse) with Turf Cutter George Innes and his assistant Sandy Brown, 1974. (*Ron Taylor Studio*)

Turf Cutter George Innes prepares to cut a turf at one of the new boundary markers, 1974. A cut turf was an important part of the ancient ceremony of sasine by which land changed ownership. (*Ron Taylor Studio*)

Town Champion John Downie followed by Squires Bobby Wilson and Eric Anderson approaching Inveresk Kirk, 1974. (*Ron Taylor Studio*)

Town Champion Bill Caird flanked by Squires Jimmy Hunter and Jimmy Arthur at Pinkie House, 1956. (*C. & F. McKean*)

Lady Esk and nymphs taking part in the Musselburgh Pageant at the racecourse, 1956. During the 1960s four of the nymphs were elected Honest Lasses. (*Ron Taylor Studio*)

Town Champion W. Aitken with Baillie Smith, holding his wand of office, and Cllr Bourhill, outside what is now Loretto Nippers School in North High Street, 1893.

Bisset Builders' float outside Balcarres House in Millhill, 1893.

Fishwives preparing for the 'Life of the Town' parade which is an integral part of the celebrations. The 1914 Riding of the Marches was postponed until after the First World War and was held in 1919.

J. & W. Stuart display 'scotch weave' nets and twines on their float, 1935.

Opposite, above: Sir Harry Lauder (right) with his niece and Mr Sandilands (left, nearest the camera), 1935. Harry Lauder was apprenticed to Sandilands Joiners in Inveresk and remained friendly with the family.

Opposite, below: Fishwives on Clark Brothers fishmongers' float, 1935. Simon Clark is standing on the left of the group at the front of the lorry. The shop at Fisherrow harbour is now operated by his son Davie and grandson Simon.

Whitelaw's Brewery offices in North High Street decorated for the Riding of the Marches with their float ready for the parade, 1935.

Provost Reid and the Baillies Hill, Lowe and Lannan, accompanied by the Town Clerk, David Taylor, returning along Linkfield Road after witnessing and recording the turf cutting at the Ravensheugh Burn, 1956.

The Ancient Order of Foresters at the junction of Bridge Street and Eskside West, 1956. A new block of flats has since been erected on this corner site.

Local market gardeners Lowes of Musselburgh advertise their famous Musselburgh leeks with an imaginative display, 1956.

Inveresk papermill float, which was based on the intertwined hearts of the luckenbooth brooch, 1956.

Musselburgh Windsor Football Club float displaying trophies and Scottish 'caps', 1956.

5

The Fishermen's Walk

The Fishermen's Walk has a long and proud history, which began some 140 years ago. It was held each year in September to mark the end of the summer fishing season and the start of the winter fishing. The Walk set off from New Street in the early afternoon, led by the local fishermen with the fishwives following on and made its way through the town to Pinkie House where sports and dancing took place. The return to Fisherrow in the early evening, with the fishermen, in their navy blue guernseys and wearing their lasses' Paisley shawls, dancing arm in arm behind the band, was a great spectacle. Unfortunately, in recent years, as a result of the loss of the fishing as a major employer in Fisherrow, the future of the Walk looks very uncertain.

Led by the Fisherrow Fishermen's Association banner, the procession makes its way along North High Street to Pinkie House, 1972. (*Ron Taylor Studio*)

The office bearers with Hector Ronald of the Fisherrow Coast Mission, 1972. The medal worn by the president was presented during the Napoleonic wars by the county of Midlothian to the Fisherrow Fishermen in recognition of their offer to defend the coastline from invasion. (*Ron Taylor Studio*)

The official group at Pinkie House, where an afternoon of sports and entertainment is held, *c*. 1910.

Dancers in the grounds of Pinkie House, 1950s. (*D.C. Thomson*)

Before the start of the Walk, crowds gather in New Street to enjoy the impromptu dancing in the street. (*C. & F. McKean*)

Fishwives in their traditional 'coats' with 'kiltit' petticoats stepping it out in New Street, 1950s.

There are some 'weel kent' faces in this group of fishwives attending the Walk in the 1960s. (*Ron Taylor Studio*)

6

Musselburgh Festival

Following the success of the Riding of the Marches in 1935, a group of local people met to discuss how the real depth of feeling for the traditions of the town, so obvious at the recent Riding of the Marches, could be kept alive during the twenty-one years until the next Riding. From that meeting the Honest Toun's Association was formed and the first festival was held in 1936. The Honest Lad, Honest Lass and attendants, who are elected annually by public vote, lead the festival celebrations which consist of a week of solemn ceremonies, ride-outs and social events in July of each year.

The first executive committee of the Honest Toun's Association, 1936. Back row, left to right: Simon Clark, Baillie Archibald, George Aitken, Bob Welsh, George McNair, Bill Caird; middle row: Hon. Treasurer Archie Sullivan, Vice-President Alex Davidson, President George Colville, Hon. Secretary Alex McDonald, Honest Lad Jimmy Arthur; front row: David Wilson, Alex Maxwell, Sandy Fortune, Johnny Miller, Terence Shanley.

Election night, 1968. The Honest Lad and Lass, Bill Duncan and Moira King, acknowledge the cheers of the crowd. (*Ron Taylor Studio*)

Counting the votes in the town hall on election night, 1955.

Kirkin', 1964. The Lad and Lass, Edward Yeoman and Sylvia Gifford, and attendants accompany Provost Arthur and the Revd Sidney Adamson to the war memorial following the kirking service. At the kirking service the chaplain formally charges the Lad and Lass to uphold the reputation and traditions of the town both at home and at the many Border Common Ridings and Festivals. (*Ron Taylor Studio*)

Angela Dougal (née DiRollo), one of the founder members of the Crusader's Riding Club, reads the Crusader's charter at Fa'side, 1957. The Crusader's Riding Club was founded in 1937 in order to promote good horsemanship among the young people of the town and to support the festival ride-outs.

Past Honest Lad Rob Waterston chats to a group of young supporters at Fa'side, 1957.

The official party and friends in the grounds of Carberry Tower, 1959. (*Ron Taylor Studio*)

Young members of the Crusader's Riding Club, 1960. (*Ron Taylor Studio*)

Awaiting the return of the Riders at Eskside, 1957.

Large crowds line the harbour as the official party boards a local fishing boat to be welcomed by members of the Fisherrow fishing community, 1957.

A rousing rendition of the 'Musselburgh Song' brings the sashing ceremony to an end, 1962. During the ceremony the sashes of office are removed from the shoulders of the previous years Lad and Lass and placed on the shoulders of the current Lad and Lass to mark their formal investiture. The Honest Lad is seen here with the Burgh Flag which has been 'bussed' with his colours by the Honest Lass. (*Ron Taylor Studio*)

Proud parents take pride of place at the Mall for the sashing, 1967. (*Ron Taylor Studio*)

The first Honest Lad and Lass, Jimmy Arthur and Ina Vass, in the High Street, 1936.

Led by Chief Marshal and Past Lad David Howie, the Lad and Lass ford the Esk at the Jooglie bridge, 1966. (*Ron Taylor Studio*)

The Official Party at Fa'side Castle, 1936.

Past Lads with Honest Lad Jack Powell at Fa'side Castle, 1967. (*Ron Taylor Studio*)

Spectators throng the grandstand for the Saturday sports at the racecourse, 1950s.

The Honest Lass presenting the youngest rider's medal, 1968. (*Ron Taylor Studio*)

7

Other Processions

Musselburgh is rich in tradition. Apart from the three main secular celebrations, much of this revolves around the churches. The town also until recently had its own brass and pipe bands and they were always in attendance to lead the celebrations. Both bands have long histories of service to the town, and Musselburgh and Fisherrow Trades Band continues to play its part in the life of the town.

Dom Gregory Ould and Father McGettigan chanting the litany of the saints as they lead the procession of clergy to the consecration of Our Lady of Loretto and St Michael's Church, 1921.

One of the many renowned Corpus Christi processions under the guidance of Father Grace and Sister Teresa Our Lady of Loretto and St Michael's Church, 1950s.

Remembrance Sunday at Inveresk Kirk, 1954.

Musselburgh Pipe Band pictured in the grounds of Spring Gardens, where they rehearsed, 1928.

Musselburgh Pipe Band some thirty years later, with Spring Gardens behind. (*Colin Ramsay*)

Musselburgh and Fisherrow Trades Band leads the procession to St Michael's Kirk at Inveresk for the kirkin' of the Honest Lad and Lass, 1957. (*Ron Taylor Studio*)

An intense group of young people at the start of the Festival Fancy Dress Parade c. 1964. Radio Scotland 24 (see the little boy in the centre front) was a 'pirate' radio station broadcasting at that time. The 'parade' is one of the high points of festival week with a large number of participants of all ages and huge crowds lining the route from Newbigging by way of the Ship Inn, to New Street.

8

School Days

Musselburgh Grammar School, founded in 1835, provided until the 1950s both primary and secondary education. The school's fee-paying primary department was one of six schools feeding the 'Grammar'. A further primary school served the needs of the Roman Catholic community and pupils from that school generally attended St David's High School in Dalkeith. Until 1975 the schools in the town were administered by Midlothian County Council, then by Lothian Regional Council and most recently by East Lothian Council. Musselburgh is also home to the Loretto School, one of the best-known and most highly regarded public schools in the country.

The Burgh School, 1952.

The Honest Lad and Lass visiting the Burgh School, 1967. (*Ron Taylor Studio*)

Campie Primary School, 1949. (*J. & I. Sternstein*)

Campie Primary School football team, 1929.

Crookston School outing to Berwick-upon-Tweed, 1954.

Crookston School football team, 1951/2. The captain and goalkeeper Billy Wilson went on to play for Hibernian and Scotland.

A young pupil presents the proceeds of a collection from the school to limbless servicemen, Fisherrow School, 1919.

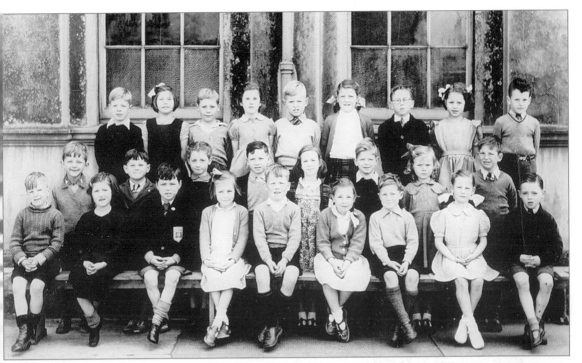

Fisherrow School, 1948. Laurie Brown, physiotherapist to the England cricket team, is fourth from the left in the middle row.

Loretto Roman Catholic Primary School, 1947.

Wallyford Primary School, 1956. (*Norman Watson*)

Wallyford Primary School, 1961. (*Norman Watson*)

Whitecraig Primary School, 1962. (*Norman Watson*)

Musselburgh Grammar School: the girls' division at the end of the nineteenth century. Musselburgh Grammar School was founded in 1835 by the town council and occupied rooms off the High Street formerly used by Miss Primrose's Ladies' School.

Musselburgh Grammar School, primary, 1943.

The Honest Lad and Lass visiting Musselburgh Grammar School, 1946.

Musselburgh Grammar School, 1953.

Musselburgh Grammar School netball squad in the early 1960s. (*J. & I. Sternstein*)

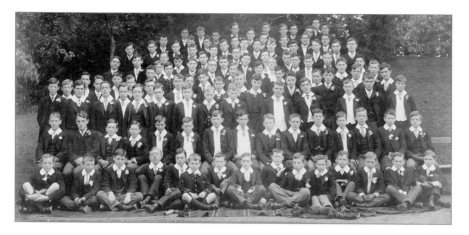

Loretto School at the end of the nineteenth century.

Loretto School band outside School House, 1895.

Loretto School rugby first XV, 1881/2. From this group came three rugby internationalists and Kenneth Mackenzie, Bishop of Argyll and the Isles.

9

Youth Organisations

In common with most other towns Musselburgh had a considerable number of uniformed organisations until the last quarter of the twentieth century when interest began to wane. The first Scout troop was registered in 1908, only one year after the movement was founded and Inveresk Kirk had its first Boys Brigade company before the First World War, although it was re-established in 1929 when the Bridge Street and North Esk churches established their companies. The first Girl Guide company was founded in 1917. At one time the town boasted 3 Scout troops, 4 Boys Brigade companies and 11 Girl Guide companies with their own Cubs, Lifeboys and Brownies. These were not the only uniformed organisations. Sea Cadets, Army Cadets and Air Cadets also flourished. The churches too had Bible classes and youth groups and some of the larger employers also provided youth-club facilities.

A group of Guiders and patrol leaders at the entrance to Fisherrow School in the late 1920s.

Boys Brigade pipe band, *c.* 1940.

The 58th Edinburgh (Inveresk) Lifeboys with the minister Dr Stiven in the manse garden, 1950s. The garden is now part of the Burgh Primary School playground.

The 58th Edinburgh (Inveresk) Lifeboys outside the church hall in Dalrymple Loan, 1950s.

Lord Provost Sir James Miller takes the salute as George Aithie leads the 51st Musselburgh Boys Brigade during a march-past in Princes Street, 1950s. (*Scotsman Publications*)

Young members of the Boys Brigade crowd round Luca's ice-cream van. The Rolls-Royce vehicle is still used by the firm on a daily basis.

The 6th Midlothian (Congregational Church) Cubs photographed on Fisherrow Links, 1950s.

The 3rd Midlothian, 1st Musselburgh Boy Scouts, 1922. This troop was founded in 1909 by a personal friend of Lord Baden-Powell. This connection led to the troop being permitted to wear the Glengarry in place of the wide-brimmed felt hat. The fashion obviously had still to catch on as only two boys are wearing the Glengarry.

The 1st Musselburgh Boy Scouts football team, league champions 1933/4. Back row, left to right: Hadden, Bourhill, Coulter, Morton, Gibson, Hunter, Henderson, Clyde; front row: ASM H. Caird, Brown, Wood, Stake, McWatt, Pow.

The 1st Musselburgh Scouts with the county flag, 1933. The flag bearers are troop leader Harry Caird and George Montgomery, with the distinctive sporran.

The 1st Musselburgh Scouts with their pipe band, which came third in the junior division of the World Pipe Band Championships.

The 3rd Musselburgh Brownies. (*C. & F. McKean*)

The Musselburgh Girl Guides in the playground of Fisherrow School, 1920s.

A group of Carberry Guides at camp, 1950s. Those pictured are Beryl Reid, Olive Johnston, Janet Higgins, Evelyn Lang, Ellen Clelland, Doreen Lang and Chrissie Beveridge. Note the large bell-tent.

Musselburgh Guides on parade passing the Central Picture House at the Mall, 1950s. (*C. & F. McKean*)

Girl Guides led by their colour party passing the Catholic church hall in Newbigging on their way to St Michael's, Inveresk.

A successful team of Sea Cadets from TS *Indefatigable* at Fisherrow harbour, 1969.

Musselburgh Squadron of the Air Training Corps at the war memorial, 1950s.

Joe Bell's Bible class at Inveresk church hall, Dalrymple Loan, 1950s.

A Congregational church youth group concert party.

A group of Sunday school teachers from the Congregational church pause to enjoy a lollipop.

Crudens' Girls' Club in the mid-1950s. The nationally known building contractors, Crudens of Musselburgh, wer for many years one of the largest employers in the town. (*Crudens Ltd*)

Musselburgh Junior Singers, *c*. 1954. This choir, in addition to entertaining locally, competed successfully i numerous music festivals, including the National Eisteddfod in Wales.

10

Mansions &
Other Buildings

Musselburgh's position, hard on the eastern boundary of Edinburgh, and its wealth, in coal, salt, fishing and manufacturing, over many centuries has left a legacy of fine historic houses of national importance and public buildings which give the town its distinctive character.

A wintry scene at the Parish Kirk of St Michael, Inveresk. The church dates from 1805 and has a beautiful contemporary plaster ceiling and some interesting stained glass. The double interlocking stairs to the balcony and to the fishermen's loft are particularly unusual. (*J.T. Knight*)

Our Lady of Loretto and St Michael of Musselburgh. The sanctuary seen here is modelled after the Holy House of Loreto, north of Ancona on the Adriatic coast of Italy. Musselburgh's links to that chapel, which was founded by crusaders returning from the Holy Land, can be traced back to 1294.

Pinkie House. The original Pinkie Tower was built in 1390 and was home to the monks of Dunfermline who controlled the local coal mining and fishing. The house was later the family home of the Hopes and is now part of Loretto School.

Newhailes House was built in 1686 and was designed by James Smith. The Dalrymple family purchased the estate in 1707 and it remained in their ownership until a few years ago when it was acquired by the National Trust for Scotland. Work has now commenced on the renovations and the house will soon be open to the public. (*Crown Copyright RCAHMS*)

Carberry Tower, 1957. This beautiful house sits in mature woods on a north-west facing site on the side of Carberry Hill where Mary Queen of Scots surrendered to the confederate lords in 1567. The house was gifted to the Church of Scotland on the death of Lady Elphinstone in 1961. (*Scotsman Publications*)

Inveresk Lodge, the former home of the Brunton family who owned the wiremills in Musselburgh, *c.* 1955. The house has been renovated by the National Trust for Scotland since this photograph was taken and the gardens are open to the public. There are interesting art nouveau features in the bedrooms and bathrooms of the main house. (*Crown Copyright RCAHMS*)

Halkerston House, *c.* 1955. The property has a unique square plan form for a house of this period, which is accentuated by the high pyramidal roof. The house has been beautifully restored and remains a family residence. (*Crown Copyright RCAHMS*)

The Manor House, Inveresk, *c.* 1955. This shows the house and the east pavilion with its ogee roof, before the reinstatement of the west pavilion which balances the new entrance gate on the axis of the front door. (*Crown Copyright RCAHMS*)

Loretto School House and the mound, which is reputed to be the site of the original Loretto chapel, built with the permission of James V by Capt John Duthie following his return to Musselburgh in 1533. The chapel was demolished in 1590 and its stones incorporated into the tolbooth.

The Drill Hall, New Street. This building once was the home of the Royal Scots Territorials but is now better known as the 'Mission'. Since the Second World War the Fisherrow Coast Mission has occupied the building, and the panels of lettering seen here have been removed.

The Musselburgh branch of Midlothian County Library was opened in 1925 and was the first branch library to be erected by any county library authority in Great Britain. On the right is the Burgh School which was demolished to make way for the Eskgreen Residential Home. (*East Lothian Council*)

The Commercial Hotel, 1937: hay and feed is being delivered to the stables at the rear of the hotel. This property, which has been sympathetically renovated as a family home, is known locally as the French Ambassador's House. (*East Lothian Council*)

This property, seen here in about 1930, in Inveresk village was for many years the home and workshop of Sandilands Joiners. In recent years it was occupied by Ritchie, the village printer, and lately has been converted to residential use.

Spring Gardens stood between The Elms and Spring Bank, now the 'Store' Club, in North High Street. Th buildings were demolished in the early 1960s and a large storage shed was erected on the New Street frontage.

Fa'side Castle, high on a hill overlooking the town, has always been a distinctive part of the local scene and played its part in the battles of Pinkie, 1547, and Prestonpans, 1745. Since its restoration as a family home the stone walls have been finished with a traditional white roughcast. (*Crown Copyright RCAHMS*)

The 'Delta' memorial, the Mall. Th President of the Old Musselburg Club each year lays a wreath at th spot in memory of the famous loc physician and writer, David McBe Moir. (*J.T. Knight*)

11

Sports

In sporting terms Musselburgh is unique, as it can claim five open golf champions, who together won the 'open' on no fewer than eleven occasions, and the Musselburgh Silver Arrow. Musselburgh Golf Club was founded in 1774 and golf had been played on the common land at Musselburgh Links for over 100 years before that date. The racecourse, which encircles the old course, was first instituted in 1816 and in recent years, thanks to a programme of rebuilding and refurbishment, has won national awards for the quality of its facilities.

The Musselburgh Silver Arrow. This trophy is reputed to be the oldest sporting trophy in the world that is still the subject of regular competition. On Musselburgh Links, in June of each year, the Royal Company of Archers, the Queen's Bodyguard in Scotland, shoot for the Arrow and the honour of adding a medal to this trophy. Although entry has been restricted to the 'Archers' since 1676, the oldest medal dates from 1603. The Musselburgh Arrow can be seen hanging vertically from the top of the spiral. (*Royal Company of Archers*)

The Royal Company of Archers in dress uniforms marching along Linkfield Road after completing another shoo c. 1960. (*Royal Company of Archers*)

Lady golfers at the first tee on Musselburgh Links, 1890. The Honourable Company of Edinburgh Golfers' Clubhous was for a time part of the old grandstand. Note the tiered seats on the side of the roof facing the racecourse. Th Honourable Company had their home at Musselburgh Links from 1874 to 1891 when they moved to Muirfield.

Golfers with their caddies with the Sea Mill and one of the many elegant clubhouses on Balcarres Road in the background. The old course hosted the world's first ladies' golf competition in 1811, when local fishwives competed for the prize of a new creel and skull and two Barcelona silk handkerchiefs.

The Mussel Bowl Golf Club. The future Provost Tom White stands behind the trophy with other prize-winners in their traditional navy-blue guernseys.

George Colville on the table green during a Musselburgh championship. George was a keen golfer and collector throughout his life, and published a number of interesting books on the history of the sport.

Left to right: James Braid, Henry Cotton, Alf Padgham and Percy Alliss during an exhibition match at the opening of Monktonhall Golf Club, 1938.

Musselburgh Golf Club, winners of the Edinburgh Summer League, 1966.

West Holmes Football Club, 1911/12, winners of the Richmond, Musselburgh and McGregor cups.

Musselburgh Union Football Club at Olivebank, at the end of a very successful season in which they won nine out of a possible thirteen trophies they competed for that year. Back row, left to right: Gillan, Wood, Fleming, Elms, Innes, Robertson, Cox; front row: Hunter, Baxter, Barnes, Rankin, McGregor, McNiell, Laing.

Musselburgh Windsor Football Club with coaches Joe Brown, Frank Ryan and Maurice Wilson. The club was founded in 1953 in the Windsor Park area of the town.

Musselburgh British Legion football team, 1959.

Musselburgh All Stars, 1967. Back row, left to right: Paterson, Cumming, Murray, Younger, Woodburn, Preston; front row: Duchart, Callaghan, G. Ormond, Spence, W. Ormond. (*Ron Taylor Studio*)

Musselburgh Rugby Football Club, 1903/4. This club predates the formation of the present club, which was established in 1921 as part of the Musselburgh Sports Club.

Musselburgh Rugby Football Club, 1935/6. Back row, left to right: McAndrew, Doig, Reid, Sinclair, Tarbet, Whitelaw, A.W. Caird, Henderson; front row: Buchanan, Smeaton, Maxwell, W. Caird, Mackie, Simpson, Learmonth.

Following election to senior membership of the Scottish Rugby Union in 1948, this seven, the next year, won the Infirmary Charity Sevens at Murrayfield in front of 12,000 spectators and the Musselburgh Sevens. They are, back row, left to right: Mooney, Fraser, Naylor, Taylor; front row: Smith, McDonald and Davidson.

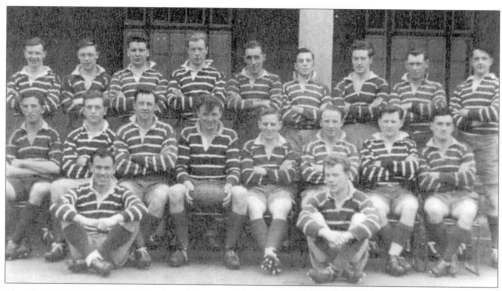

The first XV, 1956/7. Back row, left to right: Wood, Tait, Sword, Barclay-Smith, Traquair, G. Stewart, Brown, J. Stewart, Bell; front row: J. Aitken, W. Stewart, McAdam, Dodds, Smith, Thomas, McMillan, Rae; sitting on floor: Liddell, S. Aitken.

This seven from 1955 was the first seven from outside the Borders to win Kelso Sports. The club's first XV had moved four years before from the original Shirehaugh pitch to Stoneyhill which had been purchased by the town council from Inveresk Paper Company. Pictured here, back row, left to right, are: Thomas, Sword, Stewart, Rae; front row: Smith, Aitken and McMillan.

Musselburgh Grammar School hockey team, 1955/6. The members of this school team formed the Musselburgh Grammar School FP Hockey Club in 1957; it later became the Musselburgh Ladies Hockey Club. Back row, left to right: C. Lindsay, E. Jenkinson; middle row: E. Harvey, E. Ritchie, Miss Cochrane, A. Cossar, H. Clark; front row: E. Thomson, C. Allan, E. Taylor, M. Hadden, I. Wood.

Musselburgh Cricket Club, 1933. Back row, left to right: Turnbull, Mackie, D. Young, Lowe, Kilpatrick; front row: Dickson, J. Peterson, A.M. Duncan, T.H. Young, Thorburn, Aithie (sitting cross-legged); insets: H.H. Hunter, A.J. Duncan, F. Peterson.

Musselburgh Cricket Club in Lewisvale Park, 1950s.

The Papermill Badminton Club, 1950s. It was one of many clubs based around the traditional industries in the town.

Young swimmers from the Musselburgh Swimming Club and Humane Society, 1912. The club was founded in 1886 and staged 'aquatic galas' at the harbour and an annual 'round the harbour race', which continued into the 1960s.

Musselburgh Swimming Club: 1949 was a successful season for the club. As there was no public swimming pool in Musselburgh until 1995, the club used the indoor pool at Portobello.

Musselburgh Bowling Club, winners of the Midlothian Bowling Association Trophy, 1908. The club was founded in 1855, although bowling took place at Goosegreen before that date. Back row, left to right: Brown, Anderson, Rutherford, Loch, Highley, Philip; front row: Johnston, Robertson, McBean, Lowe (President), Sinclair, McKenzie.

12

Shops

This chapter is dedicated to the individual tradespeople and shopkeepers who served the community before the days of supermarkets and chain stores. Of the shops illustrated in the next few pages only Fisherrow post office, now painted light blue, and Luca's continue to trade from the same premises, while Innes the bakers in Eskside West now sports the yellow, blue and cream livery of Ford the baker. Musselburgh and Fisherrow Co-operative Society has moved to more modern premises and the remaining shops have ceased trading. The pubs have seen some changes too but have survived. Like other towns of similar size, the modern High Street is populated by banks and building societies and by local branches of supermarkets and chain stores with their standard house styles which remove much of the individual character from our main streets.

The Globe Market and Webster, newsagent, North High Street, *c.* 1920. This imposing building facing down Fisher's Wynd was radically altered in the early 1960s and the two shops combined to form the Co-op Minimarket, now Alldays.

Musselburgh & Fisherrow Co-operative Society Ltd. The 'store' occupied two similarly impressive buildings at the east end of North High Street. Long before the days of loyalty cards, the Co-op recorded all sales to members and at the end of each year the members shared in the profit generated by the society. Almost everyone had a 'store' number which was used to register purchases. The small building on the left was demolished to make way for new offices for Young's Brewery.

William Marr's grocery on the corner of Campie Road and Eskside West. It served the tenements of Mitchell Street and the council developments beyond the level crossing in Eskview.

A. Innes, bakers, Eskside West, 1935. This distinctive shopfront forming the corner of Market Street and Eskside West is still recognisable today. Since 1936 it has been owned and operated by three generations of the Ford family, and was the front shop at their Bridgend Bakery.

Brown, fishmonger, North High Street. This shop appears to have both types of window that were used to keep the fish fresh before the days of refrigerated displays, namely the opening sliding window and the fixed window with a cold-water cascade down the glass.

C. Aikman, Fisherrow post office. This beautifully detailed timber shopfront still graces the present post office in Fisherrow, although some changes have been made to the colour scheme.

I. Wilson, florist, North High Street. At the top of the Wynd, this shop is now a newsagent's. The Wilson family also owned a market garden on the west side of Lochend Road North.

Banks, fishmonger, High Street. Mrs Montgomery, left, is at the door of the shop at the bottom of the 'Fish' Close. This shop also has the distinctive fish-shop windows.

Abram Clark, grocer. This shop at 47 High Street continued as a grocery into the early 1970s and was a popular port of call for the boys from Loretto School.

J. Stagg & Son, saddlers, High Street. Jimmy Stagg is seen here at the door of his shop, which was established by his father G. Stagg, situated in the block on the east side of Newbigging. The shop also doubled as an office for the horse-drawn cabs that stood outside the shop.

Cabs at their stance in the High Street outside Jimmy Stagg's.

Luca's, Olympia Refreshment Rooms, High Street. The home of Luca's famous ice-cream still occupies this site and draws customers from all parts of the east of Scotland.

The Horseshoe, Newbigging. Jock Archibald, wearing an apron, is outside what is now the lounge bar. The false window above the door and the nameboard have since been removed and the elevation re-rendered.

The Volunteer Arms, North High Street. Known locally as 'Stagg's', it has changed little over the years and has recently won numerous awards from CAMRA and from the local press for the quality of the real ales.

The North British Railway's coach outside Flockhart's at Levenhall. This pub had one of the best sites in the town, as it stood close to the coach, and later the tram, terminus at the east end of the racecourse.

13

Social Clubs & Outings

Musselburgh has always had a large number of clubs and associations, whether attached to the churches, set up by benevolent employers or by folk with common interests. Many of these groups, like the sports clubs, have existed for over a hundred years and still form the backbone of the social life of the town.

The first committee of the Wiremill Club outside their clubrooms in Balcarres Road. This building, which has been recently restored following a fire, was the home of the Bruntsfield Links Golfing Society from 1861 to 1900.

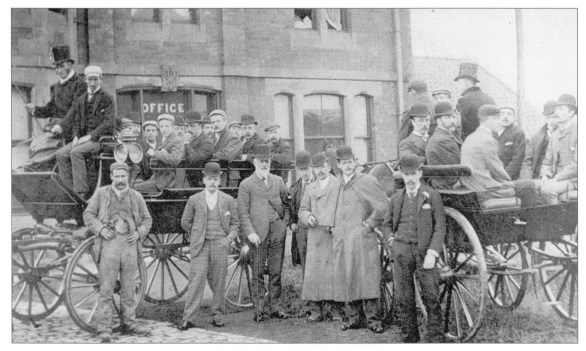

A staff outing from Brunton's wiremill to Queensferry, 1893.

Musselburgh Merchants' Association outing.

Sunday school teachers from Inveresk church, 1913.

Victory celebrations at the Papermill Club, 1945.

A break for photographs at a twenty-first birthday party at the Papermill Club, 1950s.

The St Michael's Players, 1950s. This drama group, which recently celebrated its silver jubilee, continues mount very successful productions in the Brunton Theatre.

Iembers of Musselburgh Photographic Society enjoying their fish and chips, 1926.

The Wives and Mothers Club, which met at the Stoneyhill Institute, 1949.

Musselburgh Amateur Musical Association in rehearsal for *The Mikado* with producer David Grigs and musical director Morton Robertson, 1956. The association was formed in 1950 by a few members of staff from Musselburgh and Fisherrow Co-operative Society and their friends and was originally known as the Co-operative Musical Association. Their first show, *A Country Girl*, opened in April 1951 at the Stoneyhill Institute.